One day in the summer, a cow gets out of the field. She goes to the pond for a drink of water.

She steps into the pond to have a drink. The water is cool. She goes deeper into the pond.

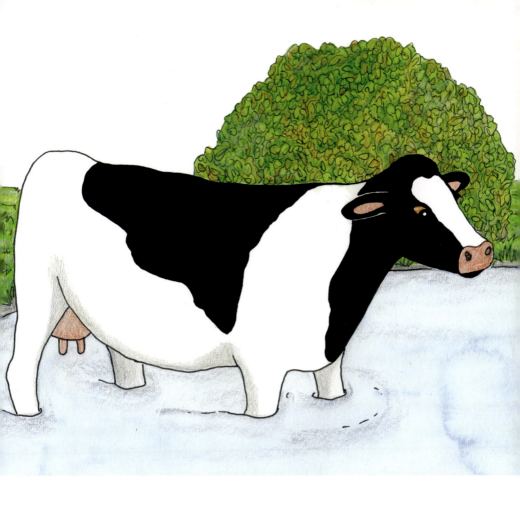

She starts to sink in the soft mud at the bottom of the pond. She gets stuck in it. 'Moo, moo, moo.'

The ducks go to see what is happening. They quack and quack for Wellington to come to the pond.

Wellington barks for Kevin to come to the pond. Then he sends Kevin to the farmyard to fetch the farmer.

Kevin and the farmer go to the pond. The farmer sees his cow stuck in the mud. He goes back to the farmyard for the tractor.

The farmer pulls the cow out of the pond with the tractor. Then he gently pulls her back to the field.

The next day he puts a big tub in the field. He fills it with water. Now his cows can have a drink without getting stuck in the pond.